Take Back the Republic

ISBN: 1-4392-5947-X
ISBN-13: 9781439259474

To order additional copies, please contact us.
BookSurge
www.booksurge.com
1-866-308-6235
orders@booksurge.com

Take Back the Republic

An Appeal to the Citizens of the United States of America

K.O. Kraig

2009

Dedication

To the fifty-five delegates to the Constitutional Convention of 1787 who accomplished a miracle that remains the gold standard of government.

To the citizens who are willing to do the hard work required to regain power over our politicians and return sanity to Washington.

To my kids and their generation, who deserve better than the status quo.

CONTENTS

PREFACE

I am not a Republican or a Democrat. I am an Independent. When I registered to vote at 18, I was a "fence rider" who was easily persuaded by both sides. So I did not declare a party (my state considers me "unaffiliated"). I am still not involved with either party, but I have definitely formed opinions about the important issues that face our nation today: skyrocketing debt and blatant corruption.

I am not a writer. But I wrote this book because I know that something needs to be done to correct the direction of our country. I find myself ashamed of my elected officials. I am angered by the corruption that permeates our politicians. I feel that our representatives have their constituents on mute. We now have a government-run government that is growing out of control. We need to return to a people-run government with politicians answering to us, not special interests. The problems facing our nation are unprecedented, but too few of our elected officials have the guts to try to fix them.

I am not a historian or lawyer. I did my best to sort out complicated issues like the stimulus bills.

If our legislators don't read the bills (which many admit to be the case) because they are too complicated, how can average citizens be expected to understand them? I will just say that I did my best.

I am not a political activist. I am just an average citizen. I am a parent who wants to leave this country a better place than it is right now, in 2009. I am speaking for myself and any other American who wants our government back. We are at a crossroads where we must either continue the status quo or make extraordinary efforts to win back our republic. I refuse to settle for the status quo.

I am not rich, but I funded this publication myself because I know the message is important. I am angry at my politicians, and I am not alone. I feel powerless in a government that was built for the people to govern. So I started looking for ways to get the power back to the people. Everyone who believes that politics has gotten out of control has a duty to do something to fix the situation. This something may be different for everyone, but the idea is to get involved in any way that you are able.

I am not a beggar. But I am begging you to get involved in your political system. Please do not be a follower. This is not an organized movement with some leader in charge telling you how to think or feel. Be the leader of your own independent party. Be a Democrat or Republican who stands up to your party when you disagree with its leaders. Hold your politicians accountable to you. That is what this book hopes to inspire. It is time to get interested and involved with what is going on in Washington. It is time to take back the republic!

Chapter 1
THE NEW GOVERNMENT ORDER

"When once a republic is corrupted, there is no possibility of remedying any of the growing evils but by removing the corruption and restoring its lost principles; every other correction is either useless or a new evil."
Thomas Jefferson

"...our fathers brought forth on this continent, a new nation, conceived in Liberty, and dedicated to the proposition that all men are created equal." So begins the Gettysburg Address by Abraham Lincoln. At a time when our nation was facing its first crisis, Lincoln helped unify the people with these words. He ended it with a statement that makes as much sense today as it did in 1863: "...that this nation, under God, shall have a new birth of freedom—and that government of the people, by the people, and for the people shall not perish from the earth." Lincoln's concluding words are the ones I choose to begin with, because we are in a new crisis that is dividing our nation. It is a battle of ideologies between conservatives and liberals that is paralyzing our legislative and executive branches. Additionally, there is far too much influence from special interest groups and lobbyists; this is tainting the political process. We the people need to take back our government.

From Lincoln's words, written in 1863, we fast forward to where we are today in 2009 and look at how we have gotten here. Just in the past ten years, we have seen unprecedented changes in our government. Our previous president, George W. Bush, faced the worst foreign attack on US soil in our history on September 11, 2001. He took action immediately to protect the people of this country. However, some of those actions have stripped Americans of some basic freedoms. The Patriot Act allowed the government some extraordinary powers in hunting down terrorists. Our government said it was necessary but also a temporary act. In my opinion, the FBI, CIA, NSA, and the Pentagon should have every tool necessary to stop terrorists both at home and abroad. However, the Patriot Act allows too much unchecked governmental power over its citizens. It needs to be revised so that, while it continues to allow our national defense and law enforcement agencies the tools they need to protect us, it does not sacrifice our civil liberties at the same time. According to Benjamin Franklin, "Any society that would give up a little liberty to gain a little security will deserve neither and lose both."

Bush then, in July of 2008, signed the Housing and Economic Recovery Act as a reaction to a struggling economy. This first "bailout" was meant to help those with subprime mortgages refinance to more affordable government-insured mortgages (at only 90% of home value) in order to avoid foreclosure. This was also supposed to stop predatory lending practices which contributed to why so many citizens faced foreclosure. It is hard to say exactly how much this costs taxpayers, but initially it allowed the FHA (Federal Housing Authority) to guarantee $300 billion in new loans. This was not enough, though, because the economy was still in trouble. So in September 2008, he signed into law the Troubled Asset Relief Program (TARP) in order to strengthen the banking industry, which was facing collapse. TARP is providing $700 billion in government funds to purchase assets and equity from struggling financial institutions. TARP also bailed out Fannie Mae and Freddie Mac for $400 billion. That is a grand total of $1.1 trillion. In his final "bailout," President Bush granted government loans to GM and Chrysler so that they would not go bankrupt. So we the people have bailed out citizens with mortgages that they could not handle, mortgage lenders who were misleading these citizens, banks that were mismanaged, and car companies that were mismanaged.

Since Barack Obama has become president, we have seen a continuation of excessive government spending in order to save our economy. In his first days as president, he signed the American Recovery and Reinvestment Act. This 1,073 page bill gives an additional $787 billion in "stimulus" money. This bill was aimed at creating jobs, but so far our jobless numbers continue to increase. I strongly suggest that readers go to www.recovery.gov and keep a close eye on the spending of this money. The government promises complete transparency in accounting for the money. Summarizing this bill and the spending alone would fill an entire book. I will say that there may be some good spending in there, but much of it is wasteful and meaningless in the creation of jobs. My state is using some of the money to provide free breakfasts for seniors at a senior center. While this is a nice thing to do, I'm not sure how it creates jobs.

Now President Obama is working on a government healthcare program that is expected to cost $1 trillion over ten years. He wants us to believe that the cost savings under this plan will pay for the plan itself (experts disagree). He also wants us to believe this is just a way to cover those individuals who are uninsured and that it will not affect those who do have coverage. However, it is his past positions that should alarm us. At an AFL/CIO conference in 2003, Obama said, "I am a proponent of a single payer healthcare plan" and then went on, "But we may not get there immediately...." In an SEIU healthcare forum in 2007, Obama said, "My commitment is to make sure we've got universal healthcare for all Americans by the end of my first term as president." He went on to say, "But I don't think we will be able to eliminate employer-based [i.e., private] healthcare immediately. There is going to be potentially some transition process. I can envision a decade out or fifteen years out or twenty years out." So when he says in 2009, "This is not a government takeover of healthcare," it begs the question: is he lying to us now or was he lying to the union groups he was speaking to before he became president? He has plainly stated in the past that his goal is to create a single payer (government controlled) system and that he will accomplish that by putting private insurance companies out of business over time. This bill is the stepping stone to 100 percent government-run healthcare for all citizens. He tells us that we can keep our private insurance, but he stops short of saying this will always be the case. There are some who support single payer, government run healthcare, but this is a time tested mistake. Under a government plan, healthcare costs will increase because our government can not manage a program of this size (approximately one-sixth of our total economy). All citizens will ultimately be responsible for paying the tab in the form of higher taxes (whether we are sick or not). Reminder: More government spending equals higher taxes. There is no way around it, so don't be convinced otherwise.

Although many of these "stimulus" programs from both administrations are "loans" that the government expects to be repaid, their current impact on our debt is enormous. (Simply put, we are borrowing money to lend money.) Indeed, some who have collected stimulus money have already begun to repay it, but that money goes back into the TARP program and may be reallocated as Congress sees fit. There is no evidence that any of these programs are helping the economy, and the funds are being misused in many cases. In a report by Andrew Cuomo, NY attorney general, six out of nine of the largest TARP fund recipients gave out employee bonuses which exceeded their company profits. We should not have faith that the government has the ability to manage either stimulus money or the insurance business properly.

In addition to the spending programs, under Obama we are seeing our right to assemble and our freedom of speech being attacked by the highest levels of our government. For a President who made his start as a community organizer, he is doing his best to denigrate protesters who do not agree with his policy. Linda Douglass, director of communications of the White House Office of Health Reform, asked citizens to "report" any "fishy" communications pertaining to health care reform on a White House blog. Then his Deputy Chief of Staff, Jim Messina, told the Democratic senators, "If you get hit, we will punch back twice as hard." Never would I believe that a White House official would talk of "punching" opposition! These are scare tactics trying to eliminate dissent. This comment by Messina resulted in violence at several Town Hall meetings. In St. Louis, two people were arrested on suspicion of assault on a citizen handing out yellow flags with "Don't tread on me" on them. These actions should alarm you regardless of your political positions.

Our Declaration of Independence states, *"That whenever any Form of Government becomes destructive to these ends, it is the Right of the People to alter or abolish it, and to institute new Government, laying its foundation on such principles and organizing its powers in such form, as to them shall seem most likely to effect their Safety and Happiness."* Of course, Thomas Jefferson was writing this to England, but today we face a form of government that is becoming similar in the level of control and lack of representation to the one we faced under Great Britain's rule.

The reason I felt that this book was necessary is that I am fed up with our politicians and I know I am not alone. Our politicians have been steering us further and further away from our Founding Fathers' message. I am not criticizing any one administration or party for this "redirection." This has been going on for a long time, and each decade has seen subtle departures. Both Democrats and Republicans are responsible in different ways. We need the people to get bigger and the government to get smaller. We must redirect our future governments to follow the Constitution. The current operating procedures in Congress and the White House are not acceptable any longer.

This is not a book of partisan politics. In fact, it is the opposite. Both parties have failed us and our political system. Both parties are equally responsible for what we have become. I will not endorse either party and tell you what you should believe (plenty of books on both sides already offer that). My goals are to inspire citizens to stand up for our political system, to remind our elected officials that they are public servants and, finally, to energize those who are willing to step up to serve the people. The bottom line is, I hope, with your help, to take back our government.

The heart of our government is the Constitution; this is what we must trust as we redirect our political trends. This is the essence of the United States of America, and it is nonnegotiable.

This country was founded on freedom. You are, therefore, free to disagree with the contents of the Constitution. However, if you cannot accept any portion of this document, you should find a new homeland. The Constitution does not need interpretation or tweaking. It is definitive and has authority over all citizens (not the other way around).

Some parts of this book will probably make you angry. Good. I hope it makes you angry to have your rights pulled out from under you. I hope that the anger will motivate you to action.

You may not agree with everything I have to say. Again, good. But I hope that you are still willing to consider the points with an open mind.

Chapter 2
TO PROGRESS OR TO PROCEED?

"The natural progress of things is for liberty to yield and government to gain ground."
Thomas Jefferson

I used to think that "progressive" sounded pretty "hip" and "now." After all, this movement is rooted in "progress" or moving forward. The progressive movement is filled with feel-good legislation that makes us all think it will make us better as a society. However, as we move forward, we also move further from our roots. A tree is strongest at the base, which is where our Constitution lies. We have progressed ourselves out to a tall branch, and we are precariously teetering out there wondering what happened. I am now figuring this out. We bought into feel-good politics and Hollywood values. We worry more about political correctness than common sense.

One feel-good policy has been to eliminate failure and make everyone a winner whether they earned it or not. Our public schools are moving away from grades and red pens. Success does not come from winning, empty rewards and pats on the back! We need to teach our youth how to handle failure. The United States of America has a long tradition of innovative firsts and successes in every field. This is a proud part of our history—but not of our future if we eliminate the opportunity to fail. Happiness comes from accomplishments, not empty compliments. Don't let your child's school or sports team take away the great learning opportunity that comes from failure.

Additionally, Hollywood values are teaching us that our worth is measured by the car we drive, the house we live in, and the vacations we are able to take. We were willing to sink ourselves into debt to reach this "American dream." When government encouraged lenders to approve subprime mortgages in order to put people into homes regardless of their ability to keep up with payments, it became political policy. As many are now learning the hard way, debt is a nightmare when it becomes insurmountable. Our government refuses to learn this lesson and continues building budgets with enormous deficits. The US debt is already on the brink of insurmountable, and it will be the job of our kids to devise a way out. We all have an obligation to live within our means and hold our government accountable for doing the same.

This progressive movement's objective is to create a new America. I will give them the benefit of the doubt and say that they have good intentions. They think they are making positive changes to our government. We should remember though that our country was founded by Europeans who came here to escape the politics there. However, many of these progressive changes involve a very European model. Not all progress is good if it takes us full circle to pre-1776. In the words of James Madison, "The happy union of these states is a wonder; their Constitution is a miracle; their example the hope of liberty throughout the world. Woe to the ambition that would meditate the destruction of either." Though progressives may be well intentioned, it is their ambition to destroy American values, and they do so through political correctness and feel-good politics. It is OK to stand against them even at the risk of being called un-American, a racist, a communist, an angry mob, or someone clinging to a gun and religion.

Our Constitution is still an example of hope throughout the world today. It has often been said that you can judge the success of a country by the number of people standing in line to make it their home. The reason people want into the US is that the opportunities here are better than those anywhere else in the world! These opportunities exist because of our Constitution. Our government is rooted in the people's law (or common law) which is the balanced center between the rulers law (tyranny) on the left and no law (anarchy) on the right. Additionally our country is a free-market economy where everyone has an equal opportunity at success. Anyone who tells you that our country needs to look more like Europe should be encouraged to move to Europe

No more progress. We must instead proceed. According to Webster's, to proceed is "To advance, especially after interruption." We are currently being misled by progressives who want to change the character of our nation. We must end this interruption and proceed with a return to our Constitutional roots. Our future prosperity lies in our past, as we cannot proceed without it. It is radical thinking to look to the past in order to advance, but most people realize it is the wise thing to do. The Constitutional Congress achieved an incredible feat in 1787, and we all owe them a big debt of gratitude. We can repay them by strict adherence to their document.

Chapter 3
THE INDEPENDENT PARTY

"[The federal government] has legislative powers on defined and limited objects, beyond which it cannot extend its jurisdiction."
James Madison

I must be very candid and admit upfront that a movement toward an organized Independent party is not for everyone. There will always be a Republican party and a Democratic party. Each party has value and is needed for a successful country. However, many politicians have become slaves to their party's ideologies. This is the partisan politics that must end. We need moderates who are willing to leave their parties and join a party that allows them the freedom to act in step with the people and not a national committee agenda.

The two things that need to happen are that people need to stop voting strictly along party lines and we need more non-politicians to run for office. The Independent party is growing because more and more people are fed up with party politics. At the time of this publication, 40 percent of US voters are registered as Independent. That is the good news. The bad news is that the Independent party is not recognized by the Federal Election Commission (FEC). In fact, in some places, it is not even considered a party but rather the lack of a party. In my state, I am an "unaffiliated" voter, which means I have no say in the primary elections. All elections are run by the state. Elections are either controlled by the Secretary of State (affiliated with a particular party) or by the FEC (bipartisan). The problem is that the Independent voter is not included in either. So folks, it is up to us if we want our voices to be heard! Nobody else has any interest in involving the Independent party in the primary elections. (Why should they?)

The solution is to use our numbers to shatter this two-party system. This can happen through initiative and referendum (I&R). I&R is a means by which citizens can (and must) dictate legislation at the state level. We the people have the right to add legislation to a ballot for a popular vote. We can begin with reforming our elections. It should be easier for all citizens to make it onto an election ballot (run for office). Additionally, the primary elections must be "open elections" which allow all registered citizens to cast a vote (regardless of their party affiliation). If your state does not offer open primaries, write a request to your state delegate. If that does not help, it may be time to consider a citizen initiative to make it happen. For every state, the method of getting an initiative on a ballot differs. You will have to check with your state to find out how you will need to proceed. It will start with a petition, but the number of signatures needed will vary by state.

Chapter 4
NECESSARY REFORM

"He who dares not offend cannot be honest."
Thomas Paine

As I said earlier, this party is not for everyone! However, the suggestions below are my "independent" views. You and I may differ on some issues, and that is OK. I want a decentralized party. There will not be a committee for the Independent party with talking points for its members. This is the party of independent thinkers and reformers. What you read below are ideas that come from everywhere on the political spectrum. I am certain my solutions will be criticized for being naïve or overly simple, considering the complexity of the issues at hand. But I think these are sensible reforms that our government must enact immediately for the long-term survival of our republic.

1) **Flat Tax**

No more IRS, no more April 15, no more 67,000 page (and counting) tax code. I do not claim to be a financial expert, but my recommendation would be an 18 percent tax on all earned income (salary, bonus, etc.) above $25,000 per year. I would also recommend a flat tax of 20 percent on all unearned income (investments, etc.). If you invest $100 and earn 10 percent ($10.00) on that investment, you would pay $2.00 in taxes. I admit that real financial experts may have to adjust these numbers, but the simplicity of a flat tax is what we deserve and must demand!

Article 1, section 8 of the Constitution says: "The Congress shall have Power To Lay and collect Taxes, Duties, Imposts and Excises, to pay the Debt and provide for the Common Defence and general Welfare of the United States; but **Duties, Imposts and Excises shall be uniform throughout the United States....**" Any policy of taxing one class more than another or allowing loopholes in the system is wrong. A flat tax is the only uniform and fair method of taxation.

2) **Fiscal Responsibility**

I would like a law requiring the federal government to maintain a balanced budget. Every budget must include money set aside to pay down the debt (substantially). There may be times of crisis when a temporary deficit is necessary. But any budget deficit must have a time frame and plan to be repaid.

Fiscal irresponsibility of both the citizens and government caused the current financial crisis. Our politicians think nothing of submitting a budget with a huge deficit. Furthermore, they have been encouraging the same behavior in our citizens. The burden (citizen debt) to the banks proved to be too much, and many banks faced collapse. However, our government decided to run up its own debt even more by assuming this burden from both citizens (Housing and Economic Recovery Act) and banks (TARP). Making matters worse, their other solution is to print more money (i.e., devalue the currency). We will have to face high taxes to pay for the bailouts AND high inflation due to the devalued dollar! Harder times are ahead if we do not stop the madness. If we experience any "recovery" at all, it will be temporary, because we are merely robbing Peter to pay Paul and it will catch up to us. There is no free money from the government. What government spends, we pay.

3) **Campaign Finance Reform**

The goal here is to remove lobbying and special interests altogether from our government. An election should be only about winning over the citizens' votes. The reforms I propose are constraining, but campaigns are where corruption begins. I feel we must take very drastic measures to get elections under control.

I recommend no more commercial advertising (on TV or radio) by candidates. Campaigns will be limited to a four-month pre-election time frame. No donations will be permitted from individuals or companies to candidates. I suggest that all candidates receive an equal sum in government funds to set up informative websites and for campaign travel to speak directly to their constituents. If they cannot campaign with the limited resources given, they need to find a different line of work. Consider this their first test in fiscal management. I strongly encourage televised debates with questions from a moderator as well as from an audience of citizens.

Currently a promising bill is being written in the Senate. It is called the "Fair Elections Now Act," or FENA. This bill will eliminate big donors and create a public fund. Candidates will be able to accept only small individual donations of $100 or less, and the total they raise will be matched by the government fund. If you are reading this book before this bill is up for a vote, please read the bill and, if you agree with it, write your senators at www.senate. org to encourage their support. Although I am encouraged that this bill was written, I do not believe it is strong enough. First, I foresee opportunities for organizations to donate several small amounts. Second, it will make fundraising more demanding (I want our representatives working for us, not fundraising for elections). Finally, it does not level the playing field for all candidates; it gives an advantage to the candidate(s) who are able to raise the most funds.

4) **Term Limits on Congress**

Did you know that half of the senators and sixty-three of the representatives in Congress have served over thirty years? That is more then a lifetime for many voters.

Each term in the Senate is six years. So I recommend that each senator be allowed two terms (for a maximum of twelve years). Every two years, one-third of the Senate is up for re-election, since the Senate is broken into three "classes," with each class on a different election cycle. Therefore, with a different senatorial population every two years, twelve years is plenty of time to serve. But if they are not serving us, we must vote them out in six years!

Representatives serve a two-year term and they are all up for re-election at the same time. They should be able to also serve twelve years, so there would be a six-term limit for them.

5) **Eliminate Perks in Congress**

Members of Congress have the best health insurance and retirement programs of anyone in the country. I believe it is highly hypocritical for members of Congress to criticize Wall Street executives for the perks they receive.

Members of Congress have a choice of ten healthcare plans and the use of federal medical facilities; they share only 25 percent of the cost with us taxpayers. If you have health insurance through your work, ask them what percent you are paying. And I am pretty certain you do not have ten options. I believe that members of Congress must be on the same healthcare program as all other government employees. If a public option is offered, they should eliminate government participation in private insurance, and all government employees will be on the public program.

They also have an attractive retirement program that is available after just one term. I won't bore you with all the details, but I think there are a few important things to note. Although Congress shares the same retirement plan as other federal employees, their benefit is calculated on a different formula (one that is a little more generous). Their accrual rate is also higher, making it possible for them to actually earn more in retirement then their departing salary within a few years. They also have the TSP (Thrift Savings Plan) if they wish to participate. This is like a 401(k) with pre-tax member contributions and a taxpayer match (up to 5 percent). As a point of reference, all of these perks are about two to three times more generous than those available to comparably paid private-sector executives. It is possible that many of our members of Congress will collect over $5 million in taxpayer money after they leave office. (Source: National Taxpayers Union)

According to our Founding Fathers, politics was never meant to be a career. In fact, Benjamin Franklin did not think that serving in Congress should be a paying job at all. No salary might be a bit extreme, but I think the retirement program definitely must be eliminated.

6) **Energy Independence**

This has national security, environmental, and economic benefits. So what is taking us so long? This is a no-brainer!

We have the technology and resources. We have coal, nuclear power, and oil here in the US. Furthermore, we should be using more solar and wind technology. There is no silver bullet here, so let's stop waiting for the one-method fix. It will take the combined use of several resources and technologies, but it CAN and MUST be done. A country that put a man on the moon within eight years of setting the goal can achieve energy independence within half that time! This needs the same determination and dedication that our space program had in the 1960s.

7) **One Issue per Bill**

The president must sign each individual piece of legislation. No more late-night add-on programs.

We must help control the spending of our government. The president must not be faced with "throwing out the baby with the bathwater" by signing good bills with bad pork spending. This will also make the president completely accountable for each piece of legislation. (Let's face it: someone needs to be accountable in Washington, and it might as well be the president.)

8) **Federal Funding**

Government should not fund state programs, private organizations or nonprofit organizations. Like item seven above, this is aimed at eliminating pork at the federal level.

Legislators often add a state project to a federal bill in order buy votes at home. They also add spending to "pay back" campaign help. However, funding these programs with our federal tax dollars is wrong. State projects should be paid at the state level. Nonprofits should raise money from private donors (who choose to donate). Private organizations need to make money without taxpayer dollars.

I believe grant money is helpful to many important programs. However, our current system is unfair in determining which programs deserve grants. It is also important to note that there are some really great advancements taking place without a penny of taxpayer money. We the people should choose the programs we give to. Congress does not have the right to decide for us.

9) **Absolute Transparency of Government**

Barack Obama talked a lot about this during his campaign. Indeed, he signed an executive order on his first day in office addressing the issue.

But how has the president been doing on being transparent?

Conservatives will point to all of the private papers that President Obama will not release, but I do believe that those in public office still have a right to some privacy. Personally, I do not care what grades they got in college or how many times they took the bar exam. I do, however, care if they were reprimanded for cheating or other un-ethical acts. The optimism I felt when, during President Obama's first days in office, he froze the salaries of his White House senior staff was popped by the growing list of czars (or advisors) that he has appointed to his staff. Obama said of the salary freeze, "This will enable the White House to stretch its budget to get more done for the country." (Press Release by the Office of the Press Secretary available at www.whitehouse.gov). So he has usurped the funds of his senior staff to hire czars. This move is counter to the transparency idea. We really just do not know enough about these advisors or their responsibilities. Additionally, we do not have the opportunity to approve candidates for these positions, since they are outside the approval process of Congress. If you check the White House website, you will find a list of all of the president's staff members, complete with biographies. You will find no such list for his czars. It seems like there is something to hide if he will not be transparent with these positions.

The other issue is that his executive order (which is a good start) falls way short of addressing the real problems. First of all, it only applies to the White House staff (not Congress). Second, it does not do enough to eliminate the special interest influence on policy. And finally, it does not address those who break the law. Any broken law or ethics violation should result in termination of the public official (from any of the three branches) from office. The citizens of this country want and deserve absolute transparency, and that can only happen through legislative controls on their actions as public officials.

Those are the very difficult reforms that are needed in Washington. Not many (if any) of our current politicians will readily sign on to these reforms so it is our job to keep the pressure on them and demand action.

Below are some common-sense suggestions for social change. Some are the sensitive issues that nobody in Washington likes to legislate but that need to be addressed. Some people criticize these views and will call you a racist for these positions. It is a sad tactic they use to keep us from discussing things that they would rather not fix. But they must be addressed, and someone in Washington needs to have the backbone to tackle them!

1) **Education**

No person should be denied higher education for financial reasons. The government has an obligation to help all students obtain a college degree if they have earned good grades in high school but cannot afford college. A government scholarship/loan program should be established for all low-income students. Family income, student grades, and student test scores will be the ONLY factors in granting these loans (not race or ethnicity). Students would be responsible for paying back most of their education costs, without interest, to the government over a ten-year post-graduation period.

Funding public education at the primary and secondary level is the responsibility of the states. The federal government should be responsible only for setting the national curriculum guidelines. Additionally, I am a strong believer in voucher programs, because they work and provide choices to low-income families in areas where public schools are failing.

The case for vouchers: The Washington, DC Opportunity Scholarship Program. In 2004, the federal government provided 1,900 vouchers for $7,500, which is around half of the cost of educating a student in a DC public school. Since this was a federally funded program, public schools did not lose any revenue. Results are now available for this program. According to the Department of Education (DOE), students who received vouchers realized improved academic performance with just nineteen months of instruction. The DOE is also seeing significant gains in reading and math achievement in voucher programs offered in Wisconsin, North Carolina, Ohio, and New York. So with these results, you may be wondering WHY the Democrats in Congress are trying to discontinue the DC Opportunity Scholarship Program. Me, too! But it is in jeopardy in spite of the many voices speaking up for the program, including Education Secretary Arne Duncan; Secretary of the US DOE Margaret Spellings; DC Schools Chancellor Michelle Rhee; and, most important, the families receiving the vouchers. (Sources: The Heritage Foundation, *US News and World Report*, *The Washington Post*, and *USA Today*.)

This country is about freedom! We deserve freedom of choice in education, too! Those who oppose vouchers are opposing our right to choose who educates our children, and that needs to change. Will there be a mass exodus from public schools? In some places, perhaps there will. If charter and private schools are doing a much better job, the public schools will see decreasing numbers. However, in many suburbs, the public schools are doing a great job. In the case of a shift in enrollment, funds will be diverted from failing schools, and the government will actually SAVE money. Bad public schools may even close, but don't expect anyone out there picketing or demanding that they remain open.

Education is paramount to the future of this country. But looking at ACT test scores, only around 23 percent of high school seniors in the US are reaching college readiness in all four subjects: English, math, reading, and science. My bet would be that if geography and history were tested, those scores would be even lower! This is not a success story for our public education system. We must demand better! Throwing money at the problem will not work. The federal government must rethink the curriculum guidelines and get tougher on holding public schools accountable for not achieving the minimum curriculum goals.

2) **Healthcare**

The number one thing that needs reform is cost control. But let's face it: government programs have never been successful at cutting or controlling costs. In fact, in all cases, costs were driven up with government in charge. It's not their fault. Government is already too big. They cannot control the money they spend on existing programs. Healthcare will be no different. The citizens of this country deserve better.

The second important reform that is needed is to create a "bill of rights" for the clients of private insurance. These are the good parts that are being suggested in the House of Representatives. Our rights should be as follows: we cannot be denied coverage due to a pre-existing condition;, our coverage will not be terminated due to a diagnosis; and we cannot be denied tests or treatments for any reason.

I want every citizen covered by insurance and able to receive the same preventive care and medical treatments that many Americans currently have. The quality of care our current medical system is able to provide is the envy of the world. Why would anyone want to overhaul that? During the summer, our House of Representatives set out to create an expansive (and expensive) overhaul without consulting the Republicans. This was a mistake, and many Americans are not satisfied with the bill. I am glad to see citizens taking their concerns to their elected officials. It is my hope that the politicians are listening (even though they seem to be dismissing the movement as artificial). A more bipartisan bill is being drafted in the Senate, and I think it has something to do with the discontent being seen at the August recess Town Hall meetings. Continue to fight until they get it right! Compromise is possible. It serves nobody to rush a bill without proper discussion and consideration of the effects the bill will ultimately have on our economy.

Making sure everyone has private insurance will contribute to dramatically reducing costs. Those who are not currently covered by insurance need to be so that they can be provided preventive care and will have a doctor to see when ill rather then going to the emergency room. One reason that the insurance rates keep going up is that hospitals must treat everyone, and those who are not insured often do not pay for these services. Hospitals must remain profitable, so those costs are made up for by higher prices paid by insurance companies covering insured patients. The insurance companies must then pass these high prices on to their customers by raising premiums. I do not believe in government forcing rate caps on what insurance companies can charge. Companies should be managing costs fairly to keep rates low. If a company is guilty of price gouging, they should be fined and watched for future abuse.

There are several reform measures in the current legislation that are good and necessary. I do not believe in government regulating private industry, but in some cases, companies act in a way that has a negative impact on society. In these cases, it is necessary for the government to intervene on behalf of its citizens. Since it is still in discussion, I will not dissect the current House version of the healthcare bill. I do encourage you to read the final version and get involved if you do not agree with it entirely. This issue affects EVERY American, so it must be done right.

3) **Religion**

"Congress shall make no law respecting an establishment of religion..." according to the first amendment. This is the "Freedom of Religion" and "Separation of Church and State" amendment.

I wholeheartedly agree with the first amendment! However, freedom OF religion is not the same as freedom FROM religion. Our government should not endorse any religion but they should also not endorse atheism either. Individuals have the right to worship as they see fit or not at all. But the word "God" in our Pledge of Allegiance and on our money does not endorse religion.

4) **Guns**

"...the right of the people to keep and bear Arms, shall not be infringed" according to the second amendment.

Unfortunately, this right is being "infringed" upon with a lot of governmental regulation. I personally do not like guns, and I certainly feel that gun violence needs to end. However, for all the rules that have already been imposed, things continue getting worse. That is because we do not need more laws limiting gun ownership. We need to enforce current laws with the strongest penalties for unlawful gun use. The gun is not the problem, and neither are the lawful gun owner and user. So let's not punish them. It is number two in the Bill of Rights, so I think our Founding Fathers felt it was pretty important.

5) **Immigration**

We must start by enforcing the current laws. Let me be clear that I do want people to immigrate here to work. But it must be through legal means! It is heartbreaking to hear that honest legal immigrants were on a waiting list for ten to twenty years before being allowed to immigrate here while we have an estimated twelve to twenty million people here illegally (and that is increasing each year). I think this is the best country in the world, and I want to share it with legal immigrants, as has always been our tradition. But I also want to keep it safe.

Our immigration laws should allow for a "worker" status which would not be subject to the same minimum wage laws as our citizens enjoy. These workers can then earn citizenship if they wish. Our immigration policy should also require that its workers and citizens-to-be speak English, hold employment, follow the law, and pay all applicable taxes.

The politically correct police wish to make illegal immigrants seem less like law breakers by calling them "undocumented workers." They also want you to think that illegal immigration is harmless. But that is not the case. Illegal immigrants are a drain on our economy; we do not know who they are; and they are under no obligation to follow our laws. They work for low wages, which helps many businesses but they don't pay taxes and many send the money home (rather then spending it here and adding to our economy). When they are injured they go to the ER and get treated for free. There cannot truly be healthcare reform if we do not address the illegal immigration issue. Illegal immigrants drive up the cost of health insurance and also our auto insurance. They drive around without a license or car insurance. When they are in an accident they pay nothing and get right back behind the wheel.

Unfortunately, there are also those who are here to do harm. Cases of murder, rape, and assault by illegal immigrants are frequent enough so that we should all be concerned. Drug trafficking and gang activity are common. It is also too easy for terrorists to enter our country. Where is the government protecting the law-abiding legal citizens of the US? We must demand protection. WE MUST KNOW WHO IS IN OUR COUNTRY! Government has an obligation to: 1) build the border fence that we were promised; 2) continually deport EVERY illegal immigrant of every nationality; and 3) impose heavy fines on employers hiring illegal immigrants. Once we have expelled the illegal immigrants, we can then go to the immigration applications and allow those who have lawfully waited for citizenship to have worker or citizen status. I also think that (to be fair) the worker status and citizenship should be offered to people of all nationalities.

6) **Affirmative Action**

Sadly this started out as a necessity but that is no longer the case. Today it is insulting and must be eliminated. We should not be making any decisions (hiring, firing, promoting, accepting, etc.) based on anything but qualifications. Both ends of the spectrum, discrimination and affirmative action, breed resentment equally. When a person is hired solely to fill a quota, those who are qualified but were not considered for the job become resentful. Furthermore, it serves nobody to hire an unqualified individual.

When a person is denied a job based on race, gender, ethnic background, sexual orientation, etc., it is a violation of the law. Every citizen in this country has equal rights under the Constitution. If people believe that they were unfairly fired, demoted, or not given a job they were qualified for, they should take their case to the courts. Affirmative action is hurting race relations in this country. I want to live in a colorblind world, but that will never happen when people can point to affirmative action, rather than the proper qualifications, as the reason for someone getting a job.

Chapter 5
WHAT CAN I DO?

"Those who expect to reap the blessings of freedom must, like men, undergo the fatigues of supporting it."
Thomas Paine

Admittedly this is the most daunting of all tasks. Apathy is the fertilizer of corruption. When corruption is planted in apathetic soil, it will grow like a weed throughout the nation. Our politicians insult us and underestimate our intelligence. But they do not underestimate our lack of interest, and they have taken advantage of that for too long. It is time to stand up and do something.

I must admit that there are no easy solutions. Change will be slow. I will not claim to have the answers, because we all must strike our own paths. However, I outline suggestions below that can be done by any citizen. Each of us must find something to do that fits with our lifestyle and personality. This book is just one of my heartfelt contributions.

Let me start with the two things I would strongly discourage:

1) Doing nothing. If we sit back and don't act soon, we may look back in ten years and ask, "Why didn't I do something?" We have hope for reform now, but we must act on it before it is too late.

2) Doing something that involves aggression or violence. We must remain calm and peaceful in our demands. We can show anger in our words but not in our deeds. Aggression does more harm than good. King Arthur's "light touch" freed Excalibur after many knights had tried without success to pull it from the stone by force. It is a myth, but you get the moral.

Suggestions for action:

1) **<u>Educate yourself:</u>**

This is part of the hard work! If you are currently getting your news from one source, you are not totally informed. The network news has done a terrible job in my lifetime of delivering unbiased reporting. Some say that we now have "state-run" networks. I don't agree, but I will say that we have "ideologically run" networks. It just happens that the ideology of the press matches with the ideology of the current administration. The network news stations do not lie to you, but they do not represent both sides equally. Admittedly, they are free to report what they wish under the Constitution. But you must be savvy to the bias you are watching. Educate yourself with other sources. Listen to all perspectives with an open mind, and then decide for yourself.

Be alert to any legislative action aimed at limiting our access to free speech. Conservative views generally dominate AM radio, offering a counterweight to more liberal TV networks. However, these conservative radio stations may be at risk now by the FCC (Federal Communications Committee). Keep an eye on the FCC's thirty-one member Advisory Committee on Diversity for Communications in the Digital Age. Conservatives fear that their goal is to drive conservative talk radio out of business through fines (in the guise of offering "diversity"). This has been the past position of Mark Lloyd, the FCC Chief Diversity Officer which he outlined in a 2007 report he co-authored called "The Structural Imbalance of Political Talk Radio." Mark Lloyd also wrote a book "Prologue to a Farce: Communication and Democracy in America" where he attacks the private communications market. A free market dictates the success of television and radio programs, and freedom of speech allows programs to report any political view they wish without controls imposed by the government. Liberal radio programming has the same rights as conservative programs, so what action is needed? Any new diversity legislation or resurrection of the Fairness Doctrine (abolished by Reagan in 1987) is outrageous and frightening!

We must also read legislation and check out what our lawmakers are up to in Congress. Much of what they work on does not make it to the news programs. Bookmark the following pages on your computer: www.opencongress.org and www. congress.org. Some of these laws may have a big impact on you, so it pays to stay informed.

We need to judge our politicians on what they do rather than what they say. We listen to them and assume what they say is what they will do. However, it takes more than listening to politicians to truly know what is going on in Washington. It takes time to research how they vote on issues, but you must do so. For this information, check out www.votesmart.org, where you can search by member of Congress to see how a given member voted on every issue. My final suggestion is to trust your intuition. If something smells like a fish, do not try to convince yourself it is anything but a fish. There is far too much marketing and spin going on in Washington.

2) **Be heard:**

Write letters to your members of Congress and to the president. Sometimes I think that Congressional members don't have time to bother with emails and letters. However, we must communicate our wishes. Otherwise, how can we blame them for not better serving us? *"One man with courage is a majority,"* said Thomas Jefferson. The following websites have links to the officials' email: www.house.gov / www.senate.gov / www.whitehouse.gov .

3) **Mobilize:**

Join with others to peacefully and respectfully protest policy that could have a big impact on you. Do not let anyone tell you that expressing your opinions (even if your words express frustration) is un-American! Do not be discouraged by any opposition to your opinion trying to scare you. Do not retreat! We are in America, and your right to assemble is protected by the Constitution. As a citizen, it is your duty to make your voice heard.

4) **Vote:**

Perhaps you already do, or maybe you will be registering for the first time. Either way, this is your voice.

Voter turnout for presidential election years can get up around 60 percent but is sometimes below 50 percent. In off years (the Congressional elections that occur between presidential cycles) turnout has been as low as 35 percent. This means that, at best, just over half of our nation bothers to be heard on Election Day. There is a word for this, and that is "pathetic"!

Here is my voter advice: Be informed and always vote your heart. In every election in which an "outsider" is on the ballot, the two parties will work hard to convince you that you are throwing away your vote by voting for this candidate. That is nonsense and shows how our politicians truly do not understand what makes our republic great. They want your vote. No, they NEED your vote. If they have not earned your vote, then give it to the candidate who has. If you vote your conscience, it is never wasted.

5) **<u>Consider running for office</u>**:

We need new blood in Washington! I am calling for average citizens. The reason we have 1,000-plus-page bills in incomprehensible language (that legislators sign without reading) is that we have far too many lawyers in Congress. I do not think you need a law degree to be a good lawmaker. Our future lawmakers could be veterans, entrepreneurs, teachers, CEOs, doctors, or "stay-at-home" moms! Are you in a position in your life to fight the system? If so, consider serving the people. If you are not able to run, are you willing to vote for a Washington outsider? If so, vote your heart. Within the past year the congressional job approval ratings have been as low as 15 percent, which means that 85 percent of the citizens are unsatisfied with the job of our elected legislators. We need "everyday citizens" stepping up to become public servants for short tenures.

Unfortunately, we have allowed a ruling class to take over our country. These career politicians are no longer like us, and, therefore, do not know how to represent us. They are pampered on taxpayer and lobbyist money. They often think they are above the law. When they are caught breaking the law or committing ethical violations, the penalties are light (if any).

The current class of politicians can take their abundant retirement benefits when they get voted out of office. With any luck, they will be the last. Hopefully our next class of Congress members will be regular people, accessible to their constituents, and respectful of our tax dollars. There is a lot of work to be done. The work that needs to be done won't be easy. But I am hopeful that people of this country feel that the republic is worth the fight. I am also hopeful that the turnaround for our government will begin in the 2010 elections. Trading out politicians between parties is not the long-term solution, however. We must demand a change of culture in Washington. We must hold our Congress and president accountable to us. We must hold our judges accountable to the Constitution. We must stay involved. We must encourage, educate, and involve our youth. We must stand guard and fight off progressive change that weakens the republic. We must start now. We must never get discouraged in the tough times or complacent in the good times.

The United States of America needs YOU to stand up now and protect her. I wish all my readers well in their contributions to protecting and preserving this nation. No effort is too small! I will end this book with a line from an Aaron Tippin song that speaks volumes: *"You've got to stand for something or you'll fall for anything."* Thank you and good luck.

AFTERWORD

After reading my book, you know what makes me angry about our government. You also know that my objective is to inspire you to speak out against the corruption and waste occurring in Washington. But you may not know what inspires me. My frustration and powerlessness in restraining an out-of-control government have been an inspiration. But, more important, I have been inspired by a book that I feel should be required reading of every high school senior before graduating or obtaining a GED. The book is called *The 5,000 Year Leap: A Miracle That Changed the World* by W. Cleon Skousen. Specifically, I found great inspiration from our Founding Fathers' political insights, and I believe that these can solve the problems that we face today. In Part I of the book, "The Founders' Monumental Task: Structuring a Government with All the Power in the People," the author describes the meaning of the three-headed eagle and two wings. You must read the book to find out about the three heads (and much more). But I want to describe the two wings, since the concept is relevant to government's role in society. Wing #1 represents the "Problem Solving Wing" (also known as the wing of compassion), while wing #2 represents the "Conservation Wing." The mission of wing #1 is to fulfill the needs of everyone through government programs. However, the job of wing #2 is to protect the nation's natural resources and freedoms. Skousen writes, "Now, if both of these wings fulfill their assigned function, the American eagle will fly straighter and higher than any civilization in the history of the world." But "…if wing #1 becomes infatuated with the idea of solving all the problems of the nation regardless of the cost, and wing #2 fails to bring its power into play to sober the problem solvers with a more realistic approach, the eagle will spin off toward the left, which is tyranny." It is equally wrong for wing #2 to withhold too many resources. All things outlined in our Founders' government stressed a balance. The first is the balance of authority through Peoples Law which is between Tyranny (complete government control) on the left and Anarchy (complete control by the people) on the right. The second is balance of power through three branches of government. In 2009, the Problem Solving Wing is out of control while the Conservation Wing is asleep. We are now spinning off to a place that the Founders strongly warned us against.

Here is what I ask of you:
- Demand that your politicians commit to the reforms outlined in this book. Vote for the

candidate most likely to make the tough decisions.

- Know your history. Please read "The 5,000 Year Leap"!
- Watch your elected officials and hold them accountable.
- If you have children, teach them the fundamental principles of our Founding Fathers (you cannot count on the schools to do it). Model your love of these principles for them through your activism.
- Always remember, being an involved citizen is not just our right, it is our duty.